Table of CONTENTS

INTRODUCTION

FILIPINO INSTANT POT COOKBOOK RECIPES

Traditional & Classic Philippine Flavors Made Quick and Easy

Janine Reyes, USRN

DISCLAIMER

Hi!

Welcome to the Filipino Instant Pot Cookbook

Welcome to the Filipino Instant Pot Cookbook, where the rich flavors of Filipino cuisine meet the convenience of modern cooking! This cookbook is designed for anyone who wants to explore the vibrant world of Filipino dishes while saving time and effort in the kitchen. Whether you are a seasoned cook or just starting your culinary journey, this book will guide you through traditional and modern recipes that your family will love.

Filipino cuisine is a beautiful tapestry of flavors, influenced by various cultures and regions. From savory stews to sweet desserts, each dish tells a story and reflects the warmth of Filipino hospitality. With the Instant Pot, you can recreate these beloved recipes with ease, allowing you to spend more time enjoying meals with your loved ones and less time in the kitchen.

Author's Journey: Janine Reyes' Story

My name is Janine Reyes, and I am thrilled to share my passion for Filipino cooking with you. Born in the Philippines and raised in the United States, I have always held a deep appreciation for my heritage. Growing up, my kitchen was filled with the vibrant aromas of traditional Filipino dishes prepared by my mother. As a dialysis nurse, I understand the importance of nurturing not just the body but also the heart, and to me, cooking is a way to connect with my roots and create lasting memories with my family.

As a mother of two beautiful daughters, Katie and Lovella, I am committed to passing down the culinary traditions of my homeland. I want to inspire families to embrace their cultural heritage and create meaningful connections through cooking. The Instant Pot has been a game-changer for me, allowing me to prepare delicious meals quickly and effortlessly, even on the busiest days.

In this cookbook, you will find a collection of my favorite recipes, each one infused with love and nostalgia. I hope that as you cook these dishes, you will also create cherished memories around your own dining table.

HOW TO BEST USE THIS  Cookbook

This cookbook is structured to make your cooking experience enjoyable and straightforward. Here's how to get the most out of it:

- Explore the Recipes: Each recipe includes detailed instructions, preparation and cooking times, serving sizes, and nutritional information. Feel free to experiment with the ingredients and adapt them to your family's tastes.

- Understand the Instant Pot: If you're new to using an Instant Pot, don't worry! I've included a section that covers the basics of the appliance, including tips for cooking Filipino dishes and how to troubleshoot common issues.

- Meal Planning Made Easy: Take advantage of the meal planning tips provided in this book. You'll find suggestions for creating your own meal plans based on the recipes, helping you save time during busy weeks.

- Cultural Context and Personal Stories: Throughout the cookbook, I've interwoven personal anecdotes and cultural insights to enrich your cooking experience. These stories are meant to connect you to the dishes on a deeper level and help you appreciate the significance of each recipe.

- Engage with Your Family: Cooking is a wonderful way to spend time with loved ones. I encourage you to involve your family in the cooking process, whether it's letting your kids help with stirring or having a cooking night with friends.

Thank you for joining me on this flavorful journey through the heart of Filipino cuisine. I hope that this cookbook inspires you to explore, create, and savor the delicious dishes that have shaped my life and the lives of so many Filipinos around the world. Let's get cooking!

Understanding
THE INSTANT POT

WHY THE INSTANT POT FOR COOKING FILIPINO FOOD?

The Instant Pot has revolutionized the way we approach cooking, especially for busy families who want to enjoy delicious meals without spending hours in the kitchen. When it comes to Filipino food, the Instant Pot is an invaluable tool that allows you to prepare traditional dishes with the same depth of flavor and authenticity as time-honored methods.

Filipino cuisine often involves slow cooking, marinating, and simmering, which can be time-consuming. The Instant Pot significantly reduces cooking times while enhancing flavors through its pressure-cooking capabilities. Whether you're making hearty stews like Sinigang or creamy dishes like Adobo sa Gata, the Instant Pot helps you achieve tender meat and rich flavors in a fraction of the time. This means you can serve your favorite Filipino dishes more often, making it easier to connect with your heritage through food.

Benefits of Using an Instant Pot
FOR FILIPINO COOKING

01 TIME EFFICIENCY

The Instant Pot can cut cooking time by up to 70%, allowing you to prepare complex dishes quickly. Imagine making a flavorful Bulalo in just over an hour instead of several hours of simmering!

02 FLAVOR ENHANCEMENT

Pressure cooking retains moisture and intensifies flavors. The traditional marinating and simmering processes are replicated in a shorter time, ensuring your dishes are just as rich and delicious.

03 VERSATILITY

The Instant Pot is a multi-cooker that can sauté, steam, slow cook, and pressure cook. This versatility means you can prepare a wide range of Filipino dishes—from soups and stews to rice and desserts—all in one appliance.

04 ENERGY EFFICIENCY

Cooking in an Instant Pot uses less energy compared to traditional stovetop cooking, making it an environmentally friendly choice as well.

05 EASE OF USE

With pre-set cooking programs and a user-friendly interface, the Instant Pot simplifies meal preparation. You can set it and forget it, freeing you to focus on other tasks while your meal cooks

06 HEALTHIER COOKING

The Instant Pot allows you to cook with less oil and fat, promoting healthier eating without sacrificing flavor. You can also easily incorporate more vegetables into your meals, aligning with the Filipino tradition of using fresh produce.

Instant Pot Basics:
KEY FEATURES AND FUNCTIONS

To make the most of your Instant Pot, it's important to understand its key features and functions. Here are some of the essential components:

01 **PRESSURE COOKING**

This is the primary function of the Instant Pot, allowing you to cook food quickly by building steam pressure. Most Filipino recipes benefit from this feature, especially those that require tenderizing tough cuts of meat.

02 **SLOW COOKING**

For those times when you want to prepare meals in advance, the slow cooking function allows you to simmer dishes over several hours, perfect for traditional recipes that develop deeper flavors over time.

03 **SAUTÉ FUNCTION**

This feature lets you sauté onions, garlic, and other aromatics directly in the pot, saving you the hassle of using multiple pans. It's ideal for starting recipes like Sinigang or Pancit Canton.

04 **RICE COOKING**

The Instant Pot has a rice cooking function that ensures perfectly cooked rice every time, which is essential for serving alongside many Filipino meals.

05 **STEAMING**

This function allows you to steam vegetables, seafood, and even desserts without using additional pots. Steamed vegetables can be a great addition to your meals, maintaining their nutrients and flavors.

Instant Pot Basics:
KEY FEATURES AND FUNCTIONS

(06) KEEP WARM

After cooking, the Instant Pot can keep your food warm until you're ready to serve. This is particularly useful when preparing large family meals or when guests are arriving at different times.

(07) TIMER AND DELAY START

You can set the timer to start cooking at a later time, allowing for flexibility in meal planning. This way, you can have a hot meal ready when you come home from work or after a busy day.

Understanding these features will empower you to navigate your Instant Pot confidently and become more efficient in the kitchen. As you become familiar with the appliance, you'll discover new ways to create delicious Filipino dishes that your family will love.

FILIPINO COOKING ESSENTIALS

Essential INGREDIENTS FOR FILIPINO CUISINE

As we embark on this culinary adventure together, it's essential to become acquainted with the fundamental ingredients that make Filipino cuisine so vibrant and delicious. Each dish tells a story, and the ingredients are the characters that bring these tales to life. In **"The Modern Filipino Family Cookbook,"** you'll discover a treasure trove of flavors and textures that are not only integral to traditional recipes but can also be found in your local grocery stores or Asian markets.

01 SOY SAUCE *("SILVER SWAN"* SOY SAUCE)

A staple seasoning used in marinades, sauces, and stir-fries. It adds a savory umami flavor to dishes like Adobo and Sinigang. Silver Swan is a brand, but Filipinos can really tell if you used a different "toyo" in your adobo. For those who are gluten-sensitive, tamari is an excellent alternative that retains the same savory flavor.

02 VINEGAR (SUKA)

Various types of vinegar, such as cane vinegar, coconut vinegar, and white vinegar, are used for marinating, pickling, and as a souring agent in dishes like Sinigang and Adobo. Each type adds a unique flavor profile.

03 GARLIC (BAWANG)

Garlic is a beloved aromatic that forms the backbone of countless Filipino recipes. Its pungent flavor transforms dishes, infusing them with warmth and richness. Fresh garlic is preferred, but garlic powder can be used for convenience.

04 GINGER (LUYA)

Ginger adds a warm, spicy note to many Filipino dishes, especially in soups and stews like sinigang. It's not only flavorful but also known for its health benefits, making it a staple in comfort foods.

Essential INGREDIENTS FOR FILIPINO CUISINE

05 COCONUT MILK (GATA)

Coconut milk is a luscious ingredient that adds creaminess and richness to dishes like kare-kare and ginataang sitaw. It's also a key component in many desserts. For a lighter version, you can use light coconut milk or even almond milk.

06 FISH SAUCE (PATIS)

Fish sauce delivers a savory, salty flavor that enhances the overall taste of dishes. It's often used as a seasoning in various recipes, including dipping sauces. If you're looking for a vegetarian alternative, consider using soy sauce or a mushroom-based sauce.

07 RICE (BIGAS)

The staple food of the Philippines, rice is served with almost every meal. Long-grain rice, jasmine rice, and sticky rice are popular choices.

08 FRESH VEGETABLES

Vegetables such as eggplant (talong), bitter melon (ampalaya), and squash (kalabasa) are staples in Filipino cooking. They add color, nutrition, and flavor to dishes, reflecting the country's agricultural bounty. Don't hesitate to experiment with seasonal vegetables available in your area.

09 OTHER HERBS AND SPICES

Slowly over the years, herbs like cilantro (wansoy) and green onions (sibuyas) are often used as garnishes or flavor enhancers in various dishes. They add freshness and brightness, elevating the overall taste. Both red and white onions are used in Filipino cuisine, providing sweetness and depth to dishes. They are often sautéed at the beginning of cooking.

Essential INGREDIENTS FOR FILIPINO CUISINE

10 CHILI PEPPERS (SILI)

Used to add heat to dishes, chili peppers can be used fresh, dried, or as a paste. They're often added to Sinigang or used as a condiment.

By familiarizing yourself with these essential ingredients, you'll be well-prepared to dive into the recipes that follow. Each ingredient not only contributes to the flavor of the dish but also connects you to the rich history and culture of the Philippines. So gather these items, and let's create culinary magic that honors the flavors of your heritage!

COMMON COOKING TECHNIQUES AND TERMS

Understanding common cooking techniques and terms used in Filipino cuisine will help you navigate recipes with ease. Here are some essential methods:

1. Sautéing *(Gisa)*: This technique involves cooking aromatics (like garlic and onion) in oil over medium heat to develop flavors before adding other ingredients. It's a foundational step in many Filipino dishes.

2. Simmering *(Pakulo)*: Simmering involves cooking food slowly in liquid at a low temperature, allowing flavors to meld. This method is often used for stews and soups like Sinigang.

3. Braised *(Pinangat)*: Braising involves cooking meat slowly in a small amount of liquid until tender. Dishes like Adobo and Humba benefit from this technique.

4. Steaming *(Pagpapasingaw)*: Steaming is a common method for cooking rice cakes (like Bibingka) and vegetables, preserving their nutrients and flavor.

5. Frying *(Prito)*: Frying, whether deep-frying or pan-frying, is used to achieve crispy textures in dishes like Lechon Kawali and Chicharrón.

6. Grilling *(Inihaw)*: Grilling adds a smoky flavor to meats and vegetables. Popular grilled dishes include Inihaw na Liempo (grilled pork belly) and Inihaw na Isda (grilled fish).

TIPS FOR ADAPTING TRADITIONAL RECIPES FOR THE INSTANT POT

Adapting traditional Filipino recipes for the Instant Pot can help you save time while still enjoying authentic flavors. Here are some practical tips:

1. Adjust Cooking Times: The Instant Pot cooks food much faster than traditional methods. Research or test cooking times for your favorite Filipino dishes to determine the right settings.

2. Sauté First: Use the sauté function to brown meat and sauté aromatics before pressure cooking. This step enhances flavors and mimics the traditional cooking process.

3. Use Natural Release for Stews: For recipes like Adobo and Sinigang, allow for a natural release after cooking. This helps the flavors meld and ensures tenderness.

4. Layer Ingredients: When cooking layered dishes, place tougher ingredients (like root vegetables) at the bottom of the pot and more delicate ingredients (like leafy greens) on top to prevent overcooking.

5. Make Use of Broth: Traditional recipes often call for water; however, using broth instead will enhance the flavor of your dishes significantly.

6. Experiment with Cooking Methods: Don't hesitate to experiment! The Instant Pot can also be used for slow cooking and sautéing, so feel free to adapt recipes based on your schedule and preferences.

7. Follow Recipes Carefully: While it's great to improvise, try to follow the initial recipes closely until you become more comfortable with the Instant Pot. This will help you understand how your ingredients behave under pressure.

8. Embrace Leftovers: The Instant Pot is perfect for repurposing leftovers. Use it to create new dishes from what you have on hand, just like traditional Filipino cooking encourages.

APPETIZERS AND SNACKS

Lumpiang Shanghai

History

Lumpiang Shanghai is one of the most popular dishes in Filipino cuisine, often served during celebrations, parties, and family gatherings. Originating from the influence of Chinese spring rolls, Lumpiang Shanghai has evolved into a uniquely Filipino favorite. It features a savory filling of ground meat, vegetables, and spices, all wrapped in a delicate, crispy shell. Today, it's a staple at birthdays, holidays, and potlucks, loved for its crunch and flavor. The dish has become a symbol of Filipino hospitality, showcasing the warmth and joy that food brings to family and friends.

Author's Personal Connection

Growing up in the Philippines, Lumpiang Shanghai was a must-have at every festive occasion. I can still picture my family gathered in the kitchen, laughter filling the air as we rolled the filling into the wrappers. My mother would always make a large batch, knowing that they would be devoured quickly. The aroma of frying spring rolls would create an irresistible temptation, making it hard to resist sneaking one before they hit the table. Now, as a mother myself, I love sharing this recipe with my daughters, passing down the love and tradition that comes with each crispy bite.

Ingredients

For the Filling
- 1 pound ground pork
- 1 cup carrots, finely grated or minced
- 1 cup green onions, finely chopped
- 1/2 cup water chestnuts, finely chopped (optional)
- 2 cloves garlic, minced
- 1 small onion, finely chopped
- 1 tablespoon soy sauce
- 1 teaspoon ground black pepper
- 1/2 teaspoon salt
- 1 tablespoon oyster sauce (optional)

For Assembly
- 20-25 spring roll wrappers
- 1 egg, beaten (for sealing)

For Frying
- Oil for frying (vegetable or canola oil)

Servings:	6-8
Preparation Time:	20 min.
Cooking Time:	15 min.
Total Time:	35 min.

Nutrition:

Calories	220
Protein	12 g
Total Fat	14 g
Saturated Fat	3 g
Cholesterol	50 mg
Carbohydrates	14 g
Dietary Fiber	1 g
Sugars	1 g
Sodium	300 mg

Instant Pot Instructions

Prepare the Filling
In a large bowl, combine ground pork, carrots, green onions, water chestnuts (if using), garlic, onion, soy sauce, black pepper, salt, and oyster sauce. Mix well until all ingredients are evenly incorporated.

Assemble the Spring Rolls
Lay a spring roll wrapper on a clean surface. Place about 2 tablespoons of the filling near the edge of the wrapper. Roll it tightly, folding in the sides as you go. Seal the edge with a bit of the beaten egg. Repeat with the remaining wrappers and filling.

Fry the Spring Rolls
Heat oil in a deep frying pan over medium heat. Carefully fry the spring rolls in batches until golden brown and crispy, about 3-4 minutes per side. Drain on paper towels to remove excess oil.

Serve
Serve hot with sweet and sour sauce, vinegar, or your favorite dipping sauce.

Kwek-Kwek

History

Kwek-Kwek is a popular Filipino street food made from quail eggs coated in a bright orange batter and deep-fried until crispy. This delightful snack is commonly sold by street vendors and is often enjoyed with a vinegar or sweet sauce for dipping. Its unique name is derived from the sound "kwek-kwek" that the eggs make when they are cooked. This dish has become a favorite among Filipinos of all ages, often served during fiestas, family gatherings, or simply enjoyed as an afternoon snack. With its crunchy exterior and savory flavor, Kwek-Kwek embodies the vibrant spirit of Filipino street food culture.

Author's Personal Connection

I have fond memories of enjoying Kwek-Kwek during my childhood in the Philippines. Street vendors would set up their stalls near schools and parks, and the sight of bright orange balls of goodness was always irresistible. My friends and I would rush to buy these tasty treats, eagerly dipping them in spicy vinegar or sweet sauce. The thrill of eating Kwek-Kwek while chatting and laughing with friends is a cherished memory I want to pass on to my daughters. Making this dish at home is a way for me to recreate those joyful moments and share the experience of Filipino street food culture with my family.

Ingredients

For the Kwek-Kwek
- 12 quail eggs, hard-boiled and peeled
- 1 cup all-purpose flour
- 1/2 cup cornstarch
- 1 teaspoon baking powder
- 1/2 teaspoon salt
- 1/2 teaspoon ground black pepper
- 1 teaspoon paprika or annatto powder (for color)
- 1 cup cold water
- Oil for frying

For Dipping Sauce
- 1/4 cup vinegar (spiced or regular)
- 1 tablespoon soy sauce
- 1 teaspoon chopped chili (optional)
- 1 tablespoon sugar (optional)

Servings:	4-6
Preparation Time:	15 min.
Cooking Time:	10 min.
Total Time:	25 min.

Nutrition:

Calories	150
Protein	6 g
Total Fat	8 g
Saturated Fat	1 g
Cholesterol	90 mg
Carbohydrates	15 g
Dietary Fiber	0 g
Sugars	1 g
Sodium	250 mg

Instant Pot Instructions

Boil the Quail Eggs
Place the trivet inside the Instant Pot and add 1 cup of water. Arrange the quail eggs on the trivet. Close the lid and set the Instant Pot to High Pressure for 3 minutes. Once done, let the pressure release naturally for 5 minutes, then perform a quick release. Transfer the eggs to an ice bath to stop the cooking process, then peel and set aside.

Cooking Instructions

Prepare the Batter
In a mixing bowl, combine the flour, cornstarch, baking powder, salt, black pepper, and paprika or annatto powder. Gradually add cold water while whisking until smooth and well combined. The batter should be thick enough to coat the eggs.

Fry the Kwek-Kwek
Heat oil in a deep frying pan over medium heat. Once hot, dip each quail egg into the batter, allowing excess to drip off, and carefully place it in the hot oil. Fry in batches, making sure not to overcrowd the pan. Fry until golden brown, about 3-4 minutes. Remove and drain on paper towels to absorb excess oil.

Prepare the Dipping Sauce
In a small bowl, mix together the vinegar, soy sauce, chopped chili (if using), and sugar (if using) to create a dipping sauce.

Serve
Serve the Kwek-Kwek hot with the dipping sauce on the side.

Chicharrón

History

Chicharrón is a beloved Filipino snack and side dish made from deep-fried pork skin, known for its irresistible crunch and savory flavor. This dish has Spanish origins and has been embraced by many cultures, including the Philippines, where it has become a staple in local cuisine. Chicharrón is often enjoyed as a crunchy snack on its own, served with vinegar for dipping, or used as a topping for other dishes like salads and soups. Its popularity today stems from its simplicity and the joyous experience of sharing it with family and friends, making it a favored choice during gatherings and celebrations.

Author's Personal Connection

I have vivid memories of enjoying Chicharrón during family gatherings and celebrations in the Philippines. The sound of the crackling pork skin as it fried in hot oil was always a sign of deliciousness to come. My family would gather around the table, eagerly waiting for the first batch to be ready, dipping the crispy pieces in vinegar or spicy sauce. It was more than just a snack; it was a moment of connection and laughter. Now, as I make this dish for my daughters, I'm reminded of those joyful times and the importance of sharing food that brings people together.

Ingredients

- 1 pound pork belly (with skin)
- 1 tablespoon salt
- 1 teaspoon ground black pepper
- 1 tablespoon vinegar
- Water (for boiling)
- Oil for frying

Servings:	4-6
Preparation Time:	15 min.
Cooking Time:	30 min.
Total Time:	45 min.

Nutrition:

Calories	300
Protein	20 g
Total Fat	25 g
Saturated Fat	8 g
Cholesterol	70 mg
Carbohydrates	0 g
Dietary Fiber	0 g
Sugars	0 g
Sodium	350 mg

Instant Pot Instructions

Prepare the Pork Belly
Cut the pork belly into 2-inch strips, keeping the skin attached. Pat dry with paper towels. Rub the salt, black pepper, and vinegar all over the pork, ensuring it's well coated.

Boil the Pork Belly
Place the pork belly strips in the Instant Pot and add enough water to cover the meat. Close the lid and set the Instant Pot to High Pressure for 30 minutes. After the cooking time is complete, allow for a natural release for 10 minutes, then perform a quick release for any remaining pressure. Remove the pork belly and let it cool slightly.

Dry the Pork Belly
Once cooled, pat the pork belly dry with paper towels. It's important to remove excess moisture to achieve maximum crispiness.

Fry the Chicharrón
Heat oil in a deep frying pan over medium-high heat. Once hot, carefully add the pork belly skin-side down. Fry until the skin is golden brown and crispy, about 5-7 minutes. You may need to fry in batches to avoid overcrowding the pan.

Drain and Cool
Remove the Chicharrón from the oil and place it on paper towels to drain excess oil. Allow it to cool slightly before serving.

Serve
Serve the Chicharrón with vinegar, soy sauce, or a spicy dipping sauce on the side.

MAIN DISHES

Chicken Adobo

History

Chicken Adobo is often regarded as the unofficial national dish of the Philippines. This flavorful stew is made by marinating chicken in a mixture of soy sauce, vinegar, garlic, and spices, then simmering until tender. The dish has Spanish roots, originating from the Spanish word "adobar," meaning "to marinate." Over time, it has evolved into numerous regional variations, showcasing the versatility of Filipino cooking. Today, Chicken Adobo is celebrated for its rich flavor and simplicity, making it a favorite among families and a must-try for anyone exploring Filipino cuisine.

Author's Personal Connection

Chicken Adobo holds a special place in my heart as it was a staple in our family meals growing up. My mother would prepare this dish on busy weekdays and special occasions alike, filling our home with its mouthwatering aroma. I remember sitting at the dining table with my family, savoring every bite and sharing stories about our day. It's a dish that brings comfort and nostalgia, and now, I love making it for my daughters, teaching them the importance of flavor and tradition in our culinary heritage. Each time I make Chicken Adobo, I feel connected to my roots and the love that comes from cooking for family.

Ingredients

- 2 pounds chicken thighs (bone-in, skin-on for more flavor)
- 1/2 cup soy sauce
- 1/2 cup white vinegar
- 1/2 cup water
- 1 head garlic, minced
- 1 onion, sliced
- 2 bay leaves
- 1 teaspoon black peppercorns
- 1 tablespoon sugar (optional, to balance acidity)
- 2 tablespoons oil (for sautéing)

Servings:	**4-6**
Preparation Time:	**10 min.**
Cooking Time:	**25 min.**
Total Time:	**35 min.**

Nutrition:

Calories	**320**
Protein	**30 g**
Total Fat	**18 g**
Saturated Fat	**5 g**
Cholesterol	**130 mg**
Carbohydrates	**5 g**
Dietary Fiber	**0 g**
Sugars	**1 g**
Sodium	**800 mg**

Instant Pot Instructions

Marinate the Chicken
In a bowl, combine soy sauce, vinegar, water, minced garlic, bay leaves, and black peppercorns. Add the chicken thighs, ensuring they are well coated. Allow to marinate for at least 15 minutes (or up to 2 hours for more flavor).

Sauté the Aromatics
Turn the Instant Pot to the Sauté function. Add the oil and sauté the sliced onion until translucent. Add the marinated chicken pieces (reserve the marinade for later) and brown for about 5 minutes on each side.

Add the Marinade
Pour the reserved marinade over the chicken. Add sugar if desired. Close the lid and set the Instant Pot to High Pressure for 10 minutes. After the cooking time is complete, allow for a natural release for 5 minutes, then perform a quick release for any remaining pressure.

Thicken the Sauce (Optional)
If you like a thicker sauce, remove the chicken and set the Instant Pot to Sauté mode again. Let the sauce simmer for a few minutes until it reduces to your desired consistency.

Serve
Serve the Chicken Adobo hot over steamed rice, spooning the sauce generously on top.

Pork Adobo

History

Pork Adobo is a classic Filipino dish that showcases the rich, savory flavors of marinated pork stewed to perfection. Like Chicken Adobo, it has Spanish origins but has evolved into a beloved staple in Filipino households. The term "adobo" refers to the marinade and cooking method, which involves soy sauce, vinegar, garlic, and spices. Each region in the Philippines has its own variation, incorporating local ingredients and flavors. Pork Adobo is often served during family gatherings and celebrations, cherished for its delicious taste and the warmth it brings to the dining table.

Author's Personal Connection

Pork Adobo is a dish that has always been a part of my family's culinary tradition. I remember my mother preparing it on weekends, filling our home with its comforting aroma. It was a dish that brought everyone together, and I loved how the flavors deepened as it simmered. Sitting at the table, I would savor each bite, often going back for seconds. Now, I enjoy making Pork Adobo for my daughters, sharing with them the joy and comfort this dish brings. It's a beautiful way to connect with my roots and create new memories around the dinner table.

Ingredients

- 2 pounds pork belly or pork shoulder, cut into 1-inch cubes
- 1/2 cup soy sauce
- 1/2 cup white vinegar
- 1 cup water
- 1 head garlic, minced
- 1 onion, sliced
- 2 bay leaves
- 1 teaspoon black peppercorns
- 1 tablespoon sugar (optional, to balance acidity)
- 2 tablespoons oil (for sautéing)

Servings:	4-6
Preparation Time:	10 min.
Cooking Time:	30 min.
Total Time:	40 min.

Nutrition:

Calories	350
Protein	30 g
Total Fat	25 g
Saturated Fat	8 g
Cholesterol	90 mg
Carbohydrates	5 g
Dietary Fiber	0 g
Sugars	1 g
Sodium	800 mg

Instant Pot Instructions

Marinate the Pork
In a bowl, combine soy sauce, vinegar, water, minced garlic, bay leaves, and black peppercorns. Add the pork cubes, ensuring they are well coated. Allow to marinate for at least 15 minutes (or up to 2 hours for deeper flavor).

Sauté the Aromatics
Turn the Instant Pot to the Sauté function. Add the oil and sauté the sliced onion until translucent. Add the marinated pork (reserve the marinade for later) and brown the meat for about 5-7 minutes.

Add the Marinade
Pour the reserved marinade over the pork. Add sugar if desired. Close the lid and set the Instant Pot to High Pressure for 15 minutes. After the cooking time is complete, allow for a natural release for 10 minutes, then perform a quick release for any remaining pressure.

Thicken the Sauce (Optional)
If you prefer a thicker sauce, remove the pork and set the Instant Pot to Sauté mode again. Let the sauce simmer for a few minutes until it reduces to your desired consistency.

Serve
Serve the Pork Adobo hot over steamed rice, spooning the sauce generously on top.

Pork Sinigang

History

Pork Sinigang is a traditional Filipino soup known for its distinctive sour flavor, typically derived from tamarind, although other souring agents like calamansi or green mango can also be used. This dish is a staple in Filipino households, especially during the rainy season, as it's believed to be comforting and nourishing. Sinigang showcases the balance of flavors that Filipino cuisine is known for, combining sour, savory, and sometimes spicy elements. It often features a variety of vegetables, making it a hearty and nutritious meal. Its popularity continues to thrive today, as families enjoy gathering around a hot bowl of Sinigang, sharing stories and laughter.

Author's Personal Connection

Pork Sinigang has always been a favorite in my family, especially on rainy days when we craved something warm and comforting. I remember my mother preparing it, carefully selecting the freshest vegetables and tamarind for that perfect sourness. The aroma of simmering pork and vegetables filled our home, making us all eagerly anticipate mealtime. Sitting around the table, we would savor the soup together, each bite reminding us of our shared heritage. Now, as I make Pork Sinigang for my daughters, I love teaching them how to appreciate the balance of flavors and the joy of cooking together. It's a dish that not only nourishes the body but also strengthens our family bonds.

Ingredients

- 2 pounds pork belly or pork shoulder, cut into 1-inch cubes
- 6 cups water
- 1 medium onion, quartered
- 2 medium tomatoes, quartered
- 1 cup tamarind paste or 1-2 cups fresh tamarind (to taste)
- 2-3 tablespoons fish sauce (patis)
- 1-2 green chili peppers (optional, for heat)
- 1 cup radish (labanos), sliced
- 1 cup eggplant, sliced
- 1 cup long green beans (sitaw), cut into 2-inch pieces
- 1 cup water spinach (kangkong) or spinach
- Salt and pepper to taste

Servings:	4-6
Preparation Time:	10 min.
Cooking Time:	30 min.
Total Time:	40 min.

Nutrition:

Calories	**320**
Protein	**25 g**
Total Fat	**20 g**
Saturated Fat	**7 g**
Cholesterol	**70 mg**
Carbohydrates	**10 g**
Dietary Fiber	**2 g**
Sugars	**2 g**
Sodium	**600 mg**

Instant Pot Instructions

Sauté the Aromatics
Turn the Instant Pot to the Sauté function. Add a small amount of oil, then sauté the onion and tomatoes until softened, about 3-5 minutes.

Add the Pork
Add the pork cubes to the pot and cook until lightly browned, about 5 minutes.

Add Water and Tamarind
Pour in the water and add the tamarind paste or fresh tamarind (if using fresh tamarind, you may want to add it whole and extract the pulp later). Stir to combine. Add the fish sauce and green chili peppers (if using).

Pressure Cook
Close the lid and set the Instant Pot to High Pressure for 25 minutes. After the cooking time is complete, allow for a natural release for 10 minutes, then perform a quick release for any remaining pressure.

Add Vegetables
Once the pressure is released, open the lid and add the radish, eggplant, and long green beans. Close the lid again and set the Instant Pot to High Pressure for an additional 5 minutes. After cooking, perform a quick release.

Finish with Water Spinach
Stir in the water spinach (kangkong) and adjust the sourness and seasoning with salt, pepper, or additional tamarind paste to taste.

Serve
Serve hot with steamed rice, allowing everyone to enjoy the rich and sour broth.

Chicken Tinola

History

Chicken Tinola is a traditional Filipino soup that features chicken, green papaya (or sayote), and a flavorful broth infused with ginger, garlic, and onion. This comforting dish is often enjoyed during family gatherings and special occasions, as it is both nourishing and delicious. Tinola has roots in Spanish culinary traditions but has evolved into a uniquely Filipino favorite, showcasing the importance of fresh ingredients and the balance of flavors in Filipino cuisine. The dish is especially loved for its soothing properties, making it a go-to meal for those feeling under the weather or during the rainy season.

Author's Personal Connection

Chicken Tinola has always been a comforting dish that I associate with family and home. My mother would often prepare it on rainy days or when someone in the family was feeling unwell. The aroma of ginger and garlic simmering in the kitchen was enough to lift anyone's spirits. I can still hear the sound of my mother chopping the vegetables and the laughter that filled our home as we gathered around the table to enjoy this warm, hearty soup. Now, as I cook Chicken Tinola for my daughters, I feel a deep sense of connection to my roots and the traditions I want to pass on. It's a dish that represents love, care, and the importance of family.

- 2 pounds beef shanks or short ribs
- 10 cups water
- 1 medium onion, quartered
- 2-3 cloves garlic, crushed
- 2-3 medium potatoes, peeled and quartered
- 1-2 ears of corn, cut into 1-inch pieces
- 1 medium head of cabbage, cut into wedges
- 2-3 tablespoons fish sauce (patis) or to taste
- 1 teaspoon black peppercorns
- Salt to taste
- Fresh cilantro or scallions for garnish (optional)

Servings:	6-8
Preparation Time:	15 min.
Cooking Time:	50 min.
Total Time:	1 hr 5 min.

Nutrition:

Calories	280
Protein	25 g
Total Fat	15 g
Saturated Fat	6 g
Cholesterol	75 mg
Carbohydrates	15 g
Dietary Fiber	3 g
Sugars	1 g
Sodium	450 mg

Instant Pot Instructions

Sauté the Aromatics
Turn the Instant Pot to the Sauté function. Add a small amount of oil (optional) and sauté the onion and garlic until fragrant, about 3-5 minutes.

Add the Beef
Add the beef shanks or short ribs to the pot and sauté for about 5 minutes, allowing them to brown slightly.

Add Water and Seasoning
Pour in the water and add the fish sauce, black peppercorns, and salt. Stir to combine.

Pressure Cook
Close the lid and set the Instant Pot to High Pressure for 40 minutes. After the cooking time is complete, allow for a natural release for 10 minutes, then perform a quick release for any remaining pressure.

Add Vegetables
Once the pressure is released, open the lid and add the potatoes and corn. Close the lid again and set the Instant Pot to High Pressure for an additional 5 minutes. After cooking, perform a quick release.

Finish with Cabbage
Stir in the cabbage and let it sit for a few minutes until wilted. Adjust seasoning if needed.

Serve
Serve hot, garnished with fresh cilantro or scallions if desired. Enjoy with steamed rice for a complete meal.

Pancit Canton

History

Pancit Canton is a popular Filipino noodle dish that has its roots in Chinese cuisine, specifically from the stir-fried noodle dishes that have been adapted and embraced in the Philippines. The term "Pancit" generally refers to noodles in Filipino, while "Canton" refers to the type of egg noodles used in this dish. Pancit Canton is often served during celebrations and special occasions, symbolizing long life and good fortune. With its colorful mix of vegetables and protein, it has become a favorite at family gatherings, showcasing the vibrant flavors and cultural fusion that characterize Filipino food.

Author's Personal Connection

Pancit Canton has always been a staple at my family's celebrations, from birthdays to holidays. I can still picture my mother in the kitchen, expertly stir-frying the noodles with an array of vegetables and meats, filling the house with an irresistible aroma. It was one of those dishes that brought everyone together, with everyone eagerly waiting to dig in. I loved how each bite was a perfect balance of flavors and textures. Now, as I prepare Pancit Canton for my daughters, I am reminded of those joyful moments and the importance of sharing meals with loved ones. It's a dish that not only fills the stomach but also warms the heart.

Ingredients

- 12 ounces Pancit Canton noodles (egg noodles)
- 2 tablespoons oil (for sautéing)
- 1 medium onion, sliced
- 4 cloves garlic, minced
- 1 medium carrot, julienned
- 1 bell pepper (red or green), sliced
- 1 cup cabbage, shredded
- 1 cup snow peas or green beans, trimmed
- 1 pound chicken breast or thigh, sliced into thin strips (or your choice of protein)
- 2 tablespoons soy sauce
- 1 tablespoon oyster sauce (optional)
- 1-2 cups chicken broth or water
- 2 green onions, chopped (for garnish)
- Salt and pepper to taste
- Lemon or calamansi wedges (for serving)

Servings:	6-8
Preparation Time:	15 min.
Cooking Time:	15 min.
Total Time:	30 min.

Nutrition:

Calories	280
Protein	18 g
Total Fat	8 g
Saturated Fat	1 g
Cholesterol	50 mg
Carbohydrates	38 g
Dietary Fiber	3 g
Sugars	2 g
Sodium	600 mg

Instant Pot Instructions

Prepare the Noodles
Soak the Pancit Canton noodles in warm water for about 10 minutes or until softened. Drain and set aside.

Sauté the Aromatics
Turn the Instant Pot to the Sauté function. Add the oil and sauté the onion and garlic until fragrant and translucent, about 2-3 minutes.

Cook the Protein
Add the sliced chicken (or your choice of protein) to the pot and cook until it's no longer pink, about 5 minutes.

Add Vegetables
Stir in the carrots, bell pepper, snow peas, and cabbage. Cook for another 2-3 minutes until the vegetables are slightly tender.

Combine Noodles and Sauce
Add the softened Pancit Canton noodles to the pot. Pour in the chicken broth (or water), soy sauce, and oyster sauce (if using). Toss everything together, ensuring the noodles are well-coated with the sauce.

Pressure Cook
Close the lid and set the Instant Pot to High Pressure for 3 minutes. After the cooking time is complete, perform a quick release.

Serve
Once the pressure is released, open the lid and gently toss the noodles. Adjust seasoning with salt and pepper to taste. Serve hot, garnished with chopped green onions and lemon or calamansi wedges on the side.

Pancit Palabok

History

Pancit Palabok is a traditional Filipino noodle dish made with rice noodles topped with a rich, savory shrimp sauce, often garnished with hard-boiled eggs, chicharrón (crispy pork skin), and green onions. The dish has roots in the Spanish influence on Filipino cuisine and is often associated with celebrations and special occasions, including birthdays and holidays. The vibrant orange color of the sauce, typically achieved with annatto powder, makes it visually appealing and festive. Pancit Palabok is not just a dish; it's a symbol of Filipino hospitality and the joy of sharing food with family and friends.

Author's Personal Connection

Pancit Palabok has always been a highlight during our family celebrations. I can still recall my mother preparing this dish with great care, making sure the shrimp sauce was perfectly seasoned and the noodles were cooked just right. The aroma of garlic and shrimp simmering on the stove would fill our home, making it hard to resist sneaking a taste before it was served. Sitting around the table with my family, enjoying Pancit Palabok, was always a joyous occasion. Now, I love making this dish for my daughters, sharing the traditions and flavors that connect us to our heritage. It's a delightful way to create new memories while honoring the old ones.

Ingredients

For the Noodles
- 12 ounces rice noodles (bihon or palabok noodles)
- 2 tablespoons oil (for sautéing)
- 1 medium onion, chopped
- 4 cloves garlic, minced
- 1 pound shrimp, peeled and deveined (reserve shells for broth)
- 2 tablespoons fish sauce (patis)
- 4 cups chicken or shrimp broth
- 2 tablespoons annatto powder (for color)
- 1 tablespoon soy sauce
- Salt and pepper to taste

For Toppings
- 3 hard-boiled eggs, sliced
- 1 cup chicharrón (crispy pork skin), crushed
- 2-3 green onions, chopped
- Lemon or calamansi wedges (for serving)

Servings:	6-8
Preparation Time:	20 min.
Cooking Time:	30 min.
Total Time:	50 min.

Nutrition:

Calories	320
Protein	20 g
Total Fat	15 g
Saturated Fat	3 g
Cholesterol	120 mg
Carbohydrates	30 g
Dietary Fiber	2 g
Sugars	1 g
Sodium	600 mg

Instant Pot Instructions

Prepare the Noodles
Soak the rice noodles in warm water for about 10-15 minutes or until softened. Drain and set aside.

Make the Shrimp Broth
Turn the Instant Pot to the Sauté function. Add a little oil and sauté the shrimp shells until fragrant, about 2-3 minutes. Add 4 cups of water and bring to a boil. Let it simmer for about 10 minutes, then strain the broth and set aside. Discard the shells.

Sauté the Aromatics
In the same pot, add 2 tablespoons of oil and sauté the chopped onion and minced garlic until fragrant and translucent, about 3-5 minutes.

Cook the Shrimp
Add the shrimp to the pot and sauté until they turn pink, about 2-3 minutes. Stir in the fish sauce.

Add Broth and Noodles
Pour in the reserved shrimp broth. Add the annatto powder and soy sauce, stirring to combine. Season with salt and pepper to taste. Bring to a boil.

Add the Noodles
Gently stir in the soaked rice noodles, making sure they are well-coated with the sauce. Close the lid and set the Instant Pot to High Pressure for 3 minutes. After the cooking time is complete, perform a quick release.

Serve
Once the pressure is released, open the lid and gently toss the noodles. Serve hot, topped with slices of hard-boiled eggs, crushed chicharrón, and chopped green onions. Offer lemon or calamansi wedges on the side for squeezing over the dish.

Lechon Kawali

History

Lechon Kawali is a beloved Filipino dish known for its crispy skin and tender, juicy meat. The name "lechon" refers to roasted or grilled meat, while "kawali" means "frying pan" in Filipino, indicating the cooking method. Traditionally, Lechon Kawali is made by boiling pork belly until tender, then deep-frying it to achieve a golden, crunchy exterior. This dish is often served during celebrations, family gatherings, and special occasions, where it is enjoyed with a side of liver sauce or vinegar dipping sauce. Its irresistible crunch and rich flavor have made it a staple in Filipino cuisine, symbolizing indulgence and celebration.

Author's Personal Connection

Lechon Kawali holds a special place in my heart, as it was always a highlight during family gatherings and festive celebrations. I remember my mother preparing this dish with great care, ensuring the pork belly was perfectly seasoned and boiled to tenderness before frying it to a glorious crisp. The sound of the oil bubbling as the pork sizzled was music to my ears, and the aroma that filled our kitchen was simply mouthwatering. Sitting around the table, everyone eagerly waiting for their first crispy bite, created an atmosphere of joy and togetherness. Now, I enjoy making Lechon Kawali for my daughters, sharing the love and tradition that come with this dish. It's a celebration of flavor and family, and I hope to pass on this cherished experience to them.

- 2 pounds pork belly
- 1 tablespoon salt
- 1 teaspoon ground black pepper
- 1 tablespoon garlic powder (optional)
- 2-3 bay leaves
- Water (for boiling)
- Oil for deep frying

Servings:	4-6
Preparation Time:	15 min.
Cooking Time:	40 min.
Total Time:	55 min.

Nutrition:

Calories	450
Protein	30 g
Total Fat	35 g
Saturated Fat	12 g
Cholesterol	80 mg
Carbohydrates	0 g
Dietary Fiber	0 g
Sugars	0 g
Sodium	600 mg

Instant Pot Instructions

Prepare the Pork Belly
Score the skin of the pork belly in a crosshatch pattern (this helps the skin become crispy). Rub the salt, black pepper, and garlic powder (if using) all over the pork belly, making sure to get it into the scores.

Boil the Pork Belly
Place the pork belly in the Instant Pot and add enough water to cover the meat. Add the bay leaves. Close the lid and set the Instant Pot to High Pressure for 30 minutes. After the cooking time is complete, allow for a natural release for 10 minutes, then perform a quick release for any remaining pressure.

Dry the Pork Belly
Remove the pork belly from the pot and pat it dry with paper towels. Let it cool slightly, then refrigerate for at least 1 hour (or overnight) to dry out the skin. This step is crucial for achieving a crispy texture.

Deep Fry the Pork Belly
In a deep frying pan or pot, heat enough oil over medium-high heat to submerge the pork belly. Once the oil is hot (about 350°F or 180°C), carefully add the pork belly, skin-side down. Fry until the skin is golden brown and crispy, about 8-10 minutes. You can turn it occasionally for even cooking.

Drain and Serve
Once crispy, remove the Lechon Kawali from the oil and drain on paper towels to remove excess oil. Let it rest for a few minutes before slicing.

Serve
Serve hot with liver sauce or a vinegar dipping sauce on the side, along with steamed rice.

Humba

History

Humba is a traditional Filipino dish originating from the Visayan region, known for its rich, sweet, and savory flavor profile. This dish features pork belly braised in a mixture of soy sauce, vinegar, and sugar, often with the addition of spices and aromatics such as garlic and bay leaves. Humba is similar to Adobo but stands out with its sweeter taste and thicker sauce. Traditionally served during special occasions and family gatherings, Humba is beloved for its melt-in-your-mouth tenderness and the way it brings people together around the dining table. It's a dish that embodies Filipino hospitality and the joy of sharing hearty meals with loved ones.

Author's Personal Connection

Humba has always been a favorite in my family, especially during festive occasions and gatherings. I remember my mother preparing this dish for special celebrations, filling our home with the mouthwatering aroma of simmering pork and spices. The way the sweet and savory sauce clung to the tender meat made every bite a delight. I loved watching her as she carefully balanced the flavors, ensuring that each ingredient complemented the others. Now, as I prepare Humba for my daughters, I feel a deep sense of nostalgia and connection to my roots. It's not just about the food; it's about the memories we create together and the importance of sharing meals as a family. I hope to pass on this cherished tradition to them, along with the love that comes with cooking.

Ingredients

- 2 pounds pork belly, cut into 1-inch cubes
- 1 tablespoon oil (for sautéing)
- 1 medium onion, sliced
- 4 cloves garlic, minced
- 1/2 cup soy sauce
- 1/4 cup vinegar
- 1/4 cup brown sugar
- 1 cup water
- 2-3 bay leaves
- 1 teaspoon black pepper
- 1/2 teaspoon salt (adjust to taste)
- 1/2 cup pineapple chunks (optional, for sweetness)

Servings:	**6-8**
Preparation Time:	**15 min.**
Cooking Time:	**1 hr**
Total Time:	**1 hr 15 min.**

Nutrition:

Calories	**400**
Protein	**25 g**
Total Fat	**30 g**
Saturated Fat	**10 g**
Cholesterol	**85 mg**
Carbohydrates	**10 g**
Dietary Fiber	**1 g**
Sugars	**5 g**
Sodium	**600 mg**

Instant Pot Instructions

Sauté the Aromatics
Turn the Instant Pot to the Sauté function. Add the oil and sauté the sliced onion and minced garlic until fragrant and the onion is translucent, about 3-5 minutes.

Brown the Pork
Add the pork belly cubes to the pot and sauté until they are lightly browned on all sides, about 5-7 minutes.

Add the Marinade
Pour in the soy sauce, vinegar, and brown sugar. Stir well to combine. Add the water, bay leaves, black pepper, and salt. If using pineapple chunks, add them at this stage as well.

Pressure Cook
Close the lid and set the Instant Pot to High Pressure for 30 minutes. After the cooking time is complete, allow for a natural release for 10 minutes, then perform a quick release for any remaining pressure.

Thicken the Sauce (Optional)
If you prefer a thicker sauce, remove the pork and set the Instant Pot to Sauté mode again. Let the sauce simmer for a few minutes until it reduces to your desired consistency.

Serve
Serve Humba hot over steamed rice, spooning the rich sauce generously on top.

Arroz Caldo

History

Arroz Caldo is a comforting Filipino rice porridge that has its roots in Chinese congee, adapted with local ingredients and flavors. Traditionally enjoyed as a breakfast dish or a soothing meal during times of illness, Arroz Caldo is made with glutinous rice simmered in chicken broth until it reaches a creamy consistency. It is typically flavored with ginger, garlic, and soy sauce, and is often topped with scallions, hard-boiled eggs, and fried garlic. This dish is beloved for its warmth and heartiness, making it a staple in Filipino households, especially during cooler months or rainy days.

Author's Personal Connection

Arroz Caldo has always been a source of comfort for me, especially during rainy days or when someone in the family was feeling under the weather. I remember my mother making this dish with love, carefully stirring the rice and broth, infusing it with ginger and garlic. The aroma wafting through our home was both soothing and inviting. Sitting down to a warm bowl of Arroz Caldo, topped with crispy garlic and fresh scallions, made me feel nurtured and cared for. Now, as I prepare Arroz Caldo for my daughters, I cherish the opportunity to share this comforting tradition and the love that comes with it. It's more than just a meal; it's a way to connect and create lasting memories together.

Ingredients

- 1 cup glutinous rice (or jasmine rice)
- 1 pound chicken (bone-in, skin-on pieces such as thighs or drumsticks)
- 6 cups chicken broth or water
- 1 medium onion, chopped
- 4 cloves garlic, minced
- 1 thumb-sized piece of ginger, sliced into thin strips
- 2-3 tablespoons fish sauce (patis)
- 1 tablespoon soy sauce (optional)
- 2-3 green onions, chopped (for garnish)
- 2 hard-boiled eggs, sliced (for topping)
- Fried garlic (for topping)
- Lemon or calamansi wedges (for serving)
- Salt and pepper to taste

Servings:	6-8
Preparation Time:	10 min.
Cooking Time:	40 min.
Total Time:	50 min.

Nutrition:

Calories	260
Protein	18 g
Total Fat	7 g
Saturated Fat	2 g
Cholesterol	70 mg
Carbohydrates	30 g
Dietary Fiber	1 g
Sugars	1 g
Sodium	600 mg

Instant Pot Instructions

Sauté the Aromatics
Turn the Instant Pot to the Sauté function. Add a small amount of oil (optional) and sauté the chopped onion, minced garlic, and ginger until fragrant and the onion is translucent, about 3-5 minutes.

Add the Chicken
Add the chicken pieces to the pot and sauté for about 5 minutes until lightly browned.

Add Rice and Broth
Stir in the glutinous rice, then pour in the chicken broth (or water) and add the fish sauce and soy sauce (if using). Stir well to combine.

Pressure Cook
Close the lid and set the Instant Pot to High Pressure for 20 minutes. After the cooking time is complete, allow for a natural release for 10 minutes, then perform a quick release for any remaining pressure.

Shred the Chicken
Once the pressure is released, open the lid and remove the chicken pieces. Shred the meat, discarding the skin and bones. Return the shredded chicken to the pot and stir until combined.

Serve
Serve Arroz Caldo hot in bowls, topped with sliced hard-boiled eggs, chopped green onions, and fried garlic. Offer lemon or calamansi wedges on the side for squeezing over the porridge.

Sopas

History

Sopas is a traditional Filipino noodle soup that is hearty and comforting, often enjoyed as a main meal or a snack. This creamy soup typically features elbow macaroni, shredded chicken, and a variety of vegetables such as carrots and cabbage, all simmered in a rich broth made creamy with the addition of evaporated milk. Sopas has Spanish roots, stemming from the word "sopa," meaning soup, and it has been adapted into a uniquely Filipino dish that embodies the warmth and hospitality of Filipino culture. It is especially popular during cooler months or rainy days, providing nourishment and comfort to families.

Author's Personal Connection

Sopas has always been one of my go-to comfort foods, especially during chilly evenings or when someone in the family was feeling under the weather. I fondly remember my mother preparing this dish, her kitchen filled with the delightful aroma of simmering chicken and vegetables. The creamy texture combined with the tender noodles created a dish that was both satisfying and soothing. Sitting around the table with my family, enjoying bowls of Sopas, made me feel nurtured and connected. Now, as I prepare Sopas for my daughters, I love sharing this comforting tradition and the love that comes with it. It's a dish that brings us together, creating memories that I hope they will cherish as much as I do.

Ingredients

- 1 pound chicken (bone-in, skin-on pieces, such as thighs or drumsticks)
- 8 cups chicken broth or water
- 1 cup elbow macaroni
- 1 medium onion, chopped
- 4 cloves garlic, minced
- 2 medium carrots, sliced
- 1 cup cabbage, chopped
- 1 cup evaporated milk
- 2-3 tablespoons fish sauce (patis)
- Salt and pepper to taste
- Chopped green onions (for garnish)
- Hard-boiled eggs, sliced (optional, for topping)

Servings:	6-8
Preparation Time:	10 min.
Cooking Time:	30 min.
Total Time:	40 min.

Nutrition:

Calories	290
Protein	20 g
Total Fat	10 g
Saturated Fat	3 g
Cholesterol	80 mg
Carbohydrates	30 g
Dietary Fiber	2 g
Sugars	2 g
Sodium	700 mg

Instant Pot Instructions

Sauté the Aromatics
Turn the Instant Pot to the Sauté function. Add a small amount of oil (optional) and sauté the chopped onion and minced garlic until fragrant and the onion is translucent, about 3-5 minutes.

Add the Chicken
Add the chicken pieces to the pot and sauté for about 5 minutes until lightly browned.

Add Broth and Cook Chicken
Pour in the chicken broth (or water) and add the fish sauce. Close the lid and set the Instant Pot to High Pressure for 15 minutes. After the cooking time is complete, allow for a natural release for 10 minutes, then perform a quick release for any remaining pressure.

Remove Chicken and Shred
Once the pressure is released, open the lid and remove the chicken pieces. Let them cool slightly, then shred the meat, discarding the skin and bones.

Cook the Macaroni
Return the shredded chicken to the pot. Stir in the elbow macaroni and carrots. Close the lid again and set the Instant Pot to High Pressure for 5 minutes. After cooking, perform a quick release.

Add Cabbage and Milk
Once the pressure is released, open the lid and stir in the chopped cabbage and evaporated milk. Season with salt and pepper to taste. Let it sit for a few minutes until the cabbage is wilted.

Serve
Serve Sopas hot in bowls, garnished with chopped green onions and slices of hard-boiled eggs if desired.

Adobo sa Gata

History

Adobo sa Gata is a delicious twist on the classic Filipino Adobo dish, incorporating coconut milk (gata) for a rich, creamy flavor. This variation is particularly popular in regions like Bicol, where coconut milk is a staple ingredient in many dishes. Adobo sa Gata retains the traditional elements of adobo—marinated meat, typically chicken or pork, simmered in vinegar and soy sauce—but the addition of coconut milk adds a luscious texture and a hint of sweetness. This comforting dish is often served over rice, making it a favorite in Filipino households for its hearty and satisfying qualities.

Author's Personal Connection

Adobo sa Gata has always been a family favorite, especially during gatherings and special occasions. Growing up, I remember the excitement in our home when my mother would prepare this dish, filling the kitchen with the enticing aroma of marinated meat simmering in coconut milk. The combination of flavors was simply irresistible, and I loved how the creamy sauce enveloped the tender meat. Sitting down to enjoy Adobo sa Gata with my family created a sense of warmth and togetherness that I cherish. Now, as I cook this dish for my daughters, I feel a deep connection to my roots and the love that comes with sharing meals. It's a way to pass on our culinary traditions and create new memories together.

VEGETARIAN & HEALTHY OPTIONS

Chickpea Adobo

History

Chickpea Adobo is a modern twist on the traditional Filipino adobo, a dish known for its savory and tangy flavors. While classic adobo is typically made with meat, this vegetarian version substitutes chickpeas, making it a hearty and nutritious option for those seeking plant-based meals. The dish retains the essential elements of adobo, including soy sauce, vinegar, garlic, and bay leaves, resulting in a deliciously rich flavor profile. Chickpea Adobo is not only a comfort food but also a testament to the adaptability of Filipino cuisine, allowing it to cater to various dietary preferences without sacrificing taste.

Author's Personal Connection

Chickpea Adobo has become a favorite in my household, especially as we embrace healthier and more plant-based meals. I appreciate how this dish retains the familiar flavors of traditional adobo while offering a nutritious alternative. I remember the first time I made this dish; the aroma of garlic and soy sauce wafting through the kitchen instantly reminded me of my childhood, sitting around the table with family enjoying classic adobo. Now, as I prepare Chickpea Adobo for my daughters, I love seeing them enjoy the same comforting flavors in a new way. This dish not only nourishes our bodies but also continues to build our connection to our culinary heritage.

Ingredients

- 2 cans (15 oz each) chickpeas, drained and rinsed
- 2 tablespoons oil (for sautéing)
- 1 medium onion, sliced
- 4 cloves garlic, minced
- 1/2 cup soy sauce
- 1/4 cup vinegar (white or cane vinegar)
- 1 cup vegetable broth or water
- 2-3 bay leaves
- 1 teaspoon ground black pepper
- Salt to taste
- 1 cup carrots, sliced (optional)
- 1 cup bell pepper, sliced (optional)
- Chopped green onions or cilantro (for garnish)

Servings:	4-6
Preparation Time:	10 min.
Cooking Time:	25 min.
Total Time:	35 min.

Nutrition:

Calories	210
Protein	10 g
Total Fat	7 g
Saturated Fat	1 g
Cholesterol	0 mg
Carbohydrates	30 g
Dietary Fiber	8 g
Sugars	2 g
Sodium	600 mg

Instant Pot Instructions

Sauté the Aromatics
Turn the Instant Pot to the Sauté function. Add the oil and sauté the sliced onion and minced garlic until fragrant and the onion is translucent, about 3-5 minutes.

Add the Chickpeas
Add the drained chickpeas to the pot and stir to combine with the aromatics.

Add the Sauce and Seasoning
Pour in the soy sauce, vinegar, vegetable broth (or water), bay leaves, and black pepper. If using, add the sliced carrots and bell pepper at this stage. Stir well to combine.

Pressure Cook
Close the lid and set the Instant Pot to High Pressure for 10 minutes. After the cooking time is complete, allow for a natural release for 5 minutes, then perform a quick release for any remaining pressure.

Adjust Seasoning
Once the pressure is released, open the lid and stir the chickpea adobo. Taste and adjust seasoning with salt if needed.

Serve
Serve hot over steamed rice, garnished with chopped green onions or cilantro.

Vegetable Stir-Fry

History

Vegetable Stir-Fry is a versatile dish in Filipino cuisine, showcasing a colorful medley of fresh vegetables cooked quickly in a hot pan, often seasoned with soy sauce or oyster sauce. This dish reflects the influence of Chinese cooking methods and ingredients, which have been embraced and adapted by Filipino cooks. Stir-frying allows the vegetables to retain their vibrant colors and nutrients, making it a healthy and quick option for busy families. Vegetable stir-fries are often served as a side dish or as a main course when paired with rice, highlighting the importance of fresh produce in Filipino meals.

Author's Personal Connection

Vegetable Stir-Fry has always been one of my go-to dishes, especially on days when I want to incorporate more vegetables into our meals. I remember my mother whipping up a quick stir-fry with whatever fresh vegetables she had on hand, creating something delicious and nutritious in just a matter of minutes. The sizzle of the vegetables in the pan and the aroma of garlic and soy sauce always made my mouth water. Now, as I prepare this dish for my daughters, I enjoy getting them involved in the kitchen, teaching them about different vegetables and how to create simple yet flavorful meals. It's a wonderful way to share the love of cooking and healthy eating while continuing the tradition of using fresh ingredients.

Ingredients

- 2 tablespoons oil (vegetable or canola)
- 4 cloves garlic, minced
- 1 medium onion, sliced
- 1 bell pepper (red or green), sliced
- 1 cup carrots, julienned
- 1 cup broccoli florets
- 1 cup snap peas or green beans, trimmed
- 1/2 cup corn (fresh or frozen)
- 2-3 tablespoons soy sauce
- 1 tablespoon oyster sauce (optional)
- Salt and pepper to taste
- Chopped green onions or sesame seeds (for garnish)

Servings:	4-6
Preparation Time:	10 min.
Cooking Time:	10 min.
Total Time:	20 min.

Nutrition:

Calories	120
Protein	3 g
Total Fat	7 g
Saturated Fat	1 g
Cholesterol	0 mg
Carbohydrates	14 g
Dietary Fiber	4 g
Sugars	3 g
Sodium	300 mg

Instant Pot Instructions

Sauté the Aromatics
Turn the Instant Pot to the Sauté function. Add the oil and sauté the minced garlic and sliced onion until fragrant and the onion is translucent, about 2-3 minutes.

Add the Vegetables
Add the bell pepper, carrots, broccoli, snap peas (or green beans), and corn to the pot. Stir-fry for about 5-6 minutes, until the vegetables are tender-crisp.

Season the Stir-Fry
Pour in the soy sauce and oyster sauce (if using). Stir well to coat the vegetables evenly. Season with salt and pepper to taste.

Serve
Turn off the Instant Pot and transfer the vegetable stir-fry to a serving platter. Garnish with chopped green onions or sesame seeds if desired.

Enjoy
Serve hot as a side dish or over steamed rice for a complete meal.

RICE AND GRAINS

Garlic Fried Rice

History

Garlic Fried Rice, or Sinangag, is a staple in Filipino cuisine, often enjoyed as a breakfast dish or as a side for lunch or dinner. This simple yet flavorful dish is made by stir-frying cooked rice with plenty of garlic, often paired with leftover meats or served alongside fried eggs. Sinangag is beloved for its aromatic flavor and is a popular choice for "silog" meals—breakfast combinations that include fried rice, a protein, and a fried egg. This dish exemplifies the Filipino knack for transforming simple ingredients into something delicious, making it a comfort food that many Filipinos cherish.

Author's Personal Connection

Garlic Fried Rice has always been a favorite in our home, especially during breakfast. I remember my mother preparing this dish with leftover rice from the night before, infusing it with the incredible aroma of sautéed garlic. The sound of garlic sizzling in the pan was music to my ears, signaling that a delicious meal was on the way. I loved pairing Sinangag with fried eggs and longganisa (Filipino sausages) or tocino (sweet cured pork). Now, as I make Garlic Fried Rice for my daughters, I enjoy teaching them the importance of using leftovers creatively while sharing the flavors and traditions that connect us to our heritage. It's a simple dish that brings back fond memories and continues to create new ones.

- 4 cups cooked rice (preferably day-old rice for best texture)
- 4 tablespoons oil (vegetable or canola)
- 6-8 cloves garlic, minced
- Salt to taste
- Pepper to taste
- Chopped green onions (for garnish, optional)

Servings:	4-6
Preparation Time:	5 min.
Cooking Time:	10 min.
Total Time:	15 min.

Nutrition:

Calories	180
Protein	4 g
Total Fat	7 g
Saturated Fat	1 g
Cholesterol	0 mg
Carbohydrates	26 g
Dietary Fiber	1 g
Sugars	1 g
Sodium	300 mg

Instant Pot Instructions

Reheat the Rice
If using freshly cooked rice, add 1/2 cup of water to the Instant Pot and place the rice in a heatproof dish on the trivet. Close the lid and set the Instant Pot to High Pressure for 5 minutes. After the cooking time is complete, perform a quick release. Alternatively, if using day-old rice, ensure it is at room temperature before cooking.

Cooking Instructions

Sauté the Garlic
Turn the Instant Pot to the Sauté function (or use a separate frying pan). Add the oil and sauté the minced garlic until golden brown and fragrant, about 2-3 minutes. Be careful not to burn the garlic.

Add the Rice
Add the cooked rice to the pot, breaking up any clumps. Stir well to combine with the garlic and oil. Sauté for about 5 minutes, allowing the rice to heat through and absorb the garlic flavor.

Season
Season with salt and pepper to taste, stirring well to distribute the seasoning evenly.

Serve
Transfer the Garlic Fried Rice to a serving dish. Garnish with chopped green onions if desired. Serve hot as a side dish or as part of a silog meal.

Coconut Rice

History

Coconut Rice, often referred to as "Nasi Lemak" in other Southeast Asian cultures, is a fragrant and flavorful dish that is a staple in Filipino cuisine as well. This dish is made by cooking rice in coconut milk, which gives it a creamy texture and a rich, aromatic flavor. In the Philippines, Coconut Rice is commonly served alongside various dishes, such as grilled meats, fried fish, or as part of a festive meal. The use of coconut milk reflects the abundant coconut trees found in the Philippines, making it an integral part of many traditional recipes. Coconut Rice is a favorite during celebrations and gatherings, showcasing the island's culinary heritage.

Author's Personal Connection

Coconut Rice has always been a special dish in our family, often prepared during special occasions or when we wanted to elevate a simple meal. I remember my mother cooking rice in coconut milk, filling our home with a delightful aroma that made our mouths water. The creamy texture of the rice, combined with its subtle sweetness, complemented any dish beautifully. Now, as I prepare Coconut Rice for my daughters, I cherish the opportunity to share this delicious tradition with them. It's a way to connect with our roots while creating new memories around the dining table.

Ingredients

- 2 cups jasmine rice (or any long-grain rice)
- 1 can (13.5 oz) coconut milk
- 1 cup water
- 1/2 teaspoon salt
- 1-2 pandan leaves (optional, for added fragrance)
- 1 tablespoon sugar (optional, for a hint of sweetness)

Servings:	4-6
Preparation Time:	5 min.
Cooking Time:	25 min.
Total Time:	30 min.

Nutrition:

Calories	220
Protein	3 g
Total Fat	9 g
Saturated Fat	8 g
Cholesterol	0 mg
Carbohydrates	34 g
Dietary Fiber	1 g
Sugars	1 g
Sodium	200 mg

Instant Pot Instructions

Rinse the Rice
Rinse the jasmine rice under cold water until the water runs clear to remove excess starch. Drain well.

Combine Ingredients
In the Instant Pot, combine the rinsed rice, coconut milk, water, salt, and sugar (if using). If you have pandan leaves, tie them in a knot and add them to the pot for added aroma.

Pressure Cook
Close the lid and set the Instant Pot to High Pressure for 6 minutes. After the cooking time is complete, allow for a natural release for 10 minutes, then perform a quick release for any remaining pressure.

Fluff the Rice
Once the pressure is released, remove the pandan leaves if used, and fluff the rice gently with a fork.

Serve
Serve Coconut Rice hot as a side dish to your favorite Filipino meals or enjoy it on its own with a sprinkle of fried garlic or fresh herbs.

DESSERTS

Leche Flan

History

Leche Flan is a traditional Filipino dessert known for its smooth and creamy texture, topped with a rich caramel sauce. This dessert has Spanish origins, derived from the Spanish "flan," but has been embraced and adapted in Filipino cuisine, often served during special occasions like birthdays, holidays, and family gatherings. Leche Flan is made with simple ingredients such as eggs, condensed milk, evaporated milk, and sugar, making it a beloved and indulgent treat. Its sweetness and silky consistency have made it a staple in Filipino celebrations, symbolizing hospitality and the joy of sharing food with loved ones.

Author's Personal Connection

Leche Flan has always been one of my favorite desserts, and I have fond memories of my mother preparing it for special occasions. I remember the excitement of watching her carefully pour the caramel sauce into the mold and then the custard mixture, hoping for that perfect, silky finish. The aroma of the flan as it baked in the oven filled our home with a sense of warmth and anticipation. Sitting down to enjoy slices of Leche Flan with my family was always a highlight, as it brought us together in celebration. Now, as I make this dessert for my daughters, I cherish the opportunity to pass down this beloved tradition and the joy that comes with sharing a sweet treat. It's a dessert that not only satisfies the sweet tooth but also connects us to our heritage.

Ingredients

For the Caramel
- 1 cup granulated sugar
- 1/4 cup water

For the Custard
- 6 large eggs
- 1 can (14 oz) sweetened condensed milk
- 1 can (12 oz) evaporated milk
- 1 teaspoon vanilla extract

Servings:	8
Preparation Time:	**15 min.**
Cooking Time:	**1 hr**
Total Time:	**1 hr 15 min.**

Nutrition:

Calories	**250**
Protein	**6 g**
Total Fat	**10 g**
Saturated Fat	**4 g**
Cholesterol	**100 mg**
Carbohydrates	**38 g**
Dietary Fiber	**0 g**
Sugars	**35 g**
Sodium	**100 mg**

Instant Pot Instructions

Prepare the Caramel
In a saucepan over medium heat, combine the sugar and water. Cook without stirring until the sugar dissolves and turns a golden amber color (about 5-10 minutes). Be careful not to burn the caramel. Immediately pour the caramel into a round mold or individual ramekins, swirling to coat the bottom evenly. Set aside to cool and harden.

Make the Custard
In a mixing bowl, whisk together the eggs, sweetened condensed milk, evaporated milk, and vanilla extract until well combined and smooth.

Pour the Custard Mixture
Carefully pour the custard mixture over the hardened caramel in the mold or ramekins.

Prepare the Instant Pot
Add 1 cup of water to the Instant Pot and place a trivet (or a steamer basket) inside. If using a round mold, cover it with aluminum foil to prevent condensation from dripping into the custard.

Pressure Cook
Place the mold on the trivet and close the lid. Set the Instant Pot to High Pressure for 25 minutes. After the cooking time is complete, allow for a natural release for 10 minutes, then perform a quick release for any remaining pressure.

Chill the Leche Flan
Carefully remove the mold from the Instant Pot and let it cool to room temperature. Once cooled, refrigerate for at least 4 hours or overnight to set.

Serve
To serve, run a knife around the edges of the flan to loosen it. Invert onto a serving plate, allowing the caramel sauce to drizzle over the top. Slice and enjoy!

Bibingka

History

Bibingka is a traditional Filipino rice cake made from rice flour and coconut milk, usually enjoyed during the Christmas season as part of the holiday festivities. Its origins can be traced back to the influence of both indigenous and Spanish culinary traditions. Bibingka is typically cooked in a clay pot lined with banana leaves, giving it a unique flavor and aroma. It is often topped with butter, grated coconut, and sometimes cheese or salted eggs, making it a deliciously sweet and savory treat. Bibingka holds a special place in Filipino culture, symbolizing community and celebration, especially during the Misa de Gallo (dawn masses) leading up to Christmas.

Author's Personal Connection

Bibingka has always been a cherished part of my family's Christmas traditions. I remember eagerly waiting for the aroma of freshly baked Bibingka to fill our home, signaling that the holiday season was upon us. My mother would prepare this delightful rice cake early in the morning, and we would often enjoy it warm, topped with butter and a sprinkle of grated coconut. Sharing Bibingka with family and friends while reminiscing about the past created a sense of joy and togetherness that I cherish. Now, as I prepare Bibingka for my daughters, I love sharing the stories and traditions that accompany this beloved treat, hoping to instill in them the same love for our culinary heritage.

Ingredients

For the Batter
- 1 cup rice flour
- 1/2 cup coconut milk
- 1/2 cup water
- 1/4 cup sugar
- 2 teaspoons baking powder
- 1/4 teaspoon salt
- 1/2 cup grated coconut (fresh or desiccated)

For Toppings
- 1/4 cup butter, melted
- 1/2 cup grated cheese (optional)
- 2-3 salted eggs, sliced (optional)
- Banana leaves (for lining)

Servings:	6-8
Preparation Time:	15 min.
Cooking Time:	25 min.
Total Time:	40 min.

Nutrition:

Calories	180
Protein	3 g
Total Fat	6 g
Saturated Fat	4 g
Cholesterol	15 mg
Carbohydrates	28 g
Dietary Fiber	1 g
Sugars	6 g
Sodium	150 mg

Instant Pot Instructions

Prepare the Banana Leaves
If using banana leaves, wilt them by passing them over an open flame or boiling water to make them pliable. Line a round cake pan (or a heatproof dish) with the banana leaves, leaving some overhang for easy removal.

Make the Batter
In a mixing bowl, combine rice flour, coconut milk, water, sugar, baking powder, and salt. Mix until smooth. Fold in the grated coconut.

Prepare the Instant Pot
Add 1 cup of water to the Instant Pot. Place a trivet or steamer basket inside the pot.

Pour the Batter
Pour the Bibingka batter into the lined cake pan. If using, place slices of salted egg and sprinkle cheese on top of the batter.

Pressure Cook
Place the cake pan on the trivet inside the Instant Pot. Close the lid and set the Instant Pot to High Pressure for 25 minutes. After the cooking time is complete, allow for a natural release for 10 minutes, then perform a quick release for any remaining pressure.

Finish and Serve
Carefully remove the cake pan from the Instant Pot. Brush the top with melted butter and let it cool slightly. If desired, you can broil it in the oven for a few minutes to achieve a golden top.

Serve
Slice and serve warm, either plain or topped with additional grated coconut and butter.

MEAL PLANNING MADE EASY

QUICK MEAL PREP TIPS FOR BUSY FAMILIES

In today's fast-paced world, finding time to prepare home-cooked meals can be a challenge. Meal planning can help simplify your cooking routine, allowing you to enjoy delicious Filipino dishes without the stress. Here are some quick meal prep tips designed for busy families:

- **Plan Your Meals:** Dedicate a few minutes each week to plan your meals. Choose recipes that can be prepared in advance or made in bulk, such as Sinigang or Adobo. This will help streamline your grocery shopping and save time during the week.

- **Create a Shopping List:** Once you've planned your meals, make a detailed shopping list based on the ingredients you'll need. Stick to the list to avoid impulse purchases and ensure you have everything on hand.

- **Batch Cooking:** Consider cooking larger portions of your favorite dishes and storing them in the refrigerator or freezer. Dishes like Pancit Canton or Chickpea Adobo can be made in bulk and reheated throughout the week.

- **Prep Ingredients Ahead of Time:** Chop vegetables, marinate meats, and measure out spices ahead of time. Store prepped ingredients in labeled containers in the refrigerator, so they are ready to use when you need them.

- **Use the Instant Pot for Batch Cooking:** Take advantage of the Instant Pot's capacity by preparing multiple servings of rice, stews, or soups at once. You can then portion them out for easy meals throughout the week.

- **Designate a Meal Prep Day:** Set aside one day a week for meal prep. Use this time to cook and portion out meals for the upcoming week. This will save you time on busy weekdays and reduce the temptation to order takeout.

- **Involve the Family:** Get your family involved in meal prep! Assign tasks to each member, such as washing vegetables, measuring ingredients, or stirring dishes. This not only makes the process faster but also fosters family bonding.

- **Utilize Leftovers Creatively:** Plan meals that can use leftovers in new ways. For example, use leftover Adobo for fried rice or transform roasted vegetables into a hearty soup.

HOW TO CREATE YOUR OWN INSTANT POT MEAL PLANS

Creating your own Instant Pot meal plans can help you maximize your cooking efficiency while enjoying a variety of delicious Filipino dishes. Here's a step-by-step guide to help you get started:

- *Choose a Theme for the Week*: Start by selecting a theme for your meal plan, such as "Meatless Meals," "Comfort Food," or "Quick Weeknight Dinners." This will help you narrow down your recipe choices and keep your meals interesting.

- *Select Recipes:* Choose a mix of recipes that can be cooked in the Instant Pot, ensuring a balance of proteins, vegetables, and grains. Aim for 5-7 recipes that can be prepared in advance or cooked quickly during the week.

- *Create a Template:* Design a simple meal planning template (either on paper or digitally) where you can outline your meals for each day of the week. Include breakfast, lunch, dinner, and snacks if desired.

- *Plan for Leftovers:* Incorporate meals that intentionally create leftovers, which can be used for lunches or repurposed into new dishes. For example, make extra Sopas to enjoy for lunch the next day.

- *Designate Cooking Days:* Identify specific days for cooking each meal. Consider using the Instant Pot for batch cooking on weekends or preparing quick meals on busier weekdays.

- *Make a Shopping List:* Based on your selected recipes, create a shopping list organized by category (produce, proteins, pantry staples, etc.). This will make grocery shopping more efficient.

HOW TO CREATE YOUR OWN INSTANT POT MEAL PLANS

- **Prep Ahead:** On your designated meal prep day, focus on washing, chopping, and marinating ingredients. You can also cook certain components (like rice or proteins) in advance to save time during the week.

- **Stay Flexible:** Life can be unpredictable, so be open to adjusting your meal plan as needed. If plans change, don't hesitate to swap out meals or use pantry staples to create something new.

- **Try New Recipes:** Incorporate new recipes into your meal plan to keep things exciting. Explore different Filipino dishes and experiment with flavors to keep your family engaged in mealtime.

- **Reflect and Adjust:** At the end of the week, take a moment to reflect on what worked well and what didn't. Adjust your meal planning approach for the following week based on your family's preferences and feedback.

By implementing these meal planning strategies, you can simplify your cooking routine and enjoy the delicious, comforting flavors of Filipino cuisine with the convenience of the Instant Pot. Happy cooking!

SHOPPING MADE SIMPLE

Essential INGREDIENTS TO STOCK FOR FILIPINO INSTANT POT COOKING

To make your Filipino cooking experience seamless and enjoyable, it's essential to have a well-stocked pantry with ingredients that are commonly used in traditional dishes. Here's a list of essential ingredients you should consider keeping on hand for Instant Pot cooking:

Pantry Staples:

- Rice: Jasmine rice or long-grain rice is a staple in Filipino households and pairs well with many dishes.

- Soy Sauce: A key seasoning for marinades, stir-fries, and sauces, soy sauce adds depth of flavor to dishes like Adobo and Sopas.

- Vinegar: Various types of vinegar (cane, coconut, white) are used for marinating and adding tanginess to dishes, especially in Sinigang and Adobo.

- Fish Sauce (Patis): This fermented condiment adds umami and saltiness to many Filipino dishes.

- Coconut Milk: Used in both savory and sweet dishes, coconut milk is essential for recipes like Adobo sa Gata and Bibingka.

- Canned Tomatoes: Useful for stews and sauces, canned tomatoes can be a great addition to recipes like Mechado.

- Sugar: Both white and brown sugar are used to balance flavors in savory dishes and for sweet treats.

- Garlic and Onions: Essential aromatics that form the base of many Filipino recipes.

- Spices: Common spices include black pepper, bay leaves, and ginger, which add flavor to various dishes.

Essential INGREDIENTS TO STOCK FOR FILIPINO INSTANT POT COOKING

Fresh Produce:

1. Vegetables: Stock up on common vegetables such as:
   - Onions: Both yellow and red varieties
   - Garlic: Fresh cloves for flavoring
   - Ginger: Adds warmth and depth to soups and stews
   - Tomatoes: Fresh for stews or salads
   - Leafy Greens: Such as spinach, water spinach (kangkong), or cabbage for soups and stir-fries
   - Root Vegetables: Carrots, potatoes, and radishes are often used in stews.

2. Fruits:
   - Banana Leaves: Used for wrapping and flavoring dishes like Bibingka.
   - Coconut: Fresh or desiccated coconut can be used in desserts and rice dishes.
   - Lemon or Calamansi: Citrus adds brightness and acidity to dishes.

Proteins:

   - Meat: Stock up on common proteins such as chicken, pork, and beef. These are often used in staples like Adobo, Sinigang, and Bulalo.

   - Seafood: Shrimp, fish, and squid can be used in a variety of Filipino dishes.

   - Legumes: Canned or dried chickpeas, lentils, and mung beans are great for vegetarian dishes like Chickpea Adobo.

Condiments and Sauces:

   - Oyster Sauce: Adds a rich flavor to stir-fries and other dishes.
   - Chili Sauce: For those who enjoy a bit of heat in their meals.
   - Soy Sauce: the right brand always matters.

WHERE TO FIND FILIPINO INGREDIENTS

Finding Filipino ingredients can sometimes be a challenge, depending on your location. Here are some tips on where to shop for these essential items:

- **ASIAN GROCERY STORES:** These stores often carry a wide variety of Filipino and other Asian ingredients. Look for sections dedicated to Filipino products, including canned goods, sauces, and dried goods.

- **FILIPINO MARKETS:** If you have a Filipino community nearby, check for local Filipino markets. These shops usually stock a broader selection of authentic Filipino ingredients and products.

- **INTERNATIONAL SUPERMARKETS:** Many larger supermarkets have an international aisle that includes ingredients from various cuisines, including Filipino staples like soy sauce, fish sauce, and canned coconut milk.

- **FARMER'S MARKET:** Fresh produce, such as vegetables and herbs, can often be found at local farmers' markets. This is a great way to source fresh, high-quality ingredients for your dishes.

- **ONLINE GROCERY STORES:** Websites like Amazon and specialized online Filipino grocery stores offer a wide selection of ingredients that can be delivered to your doorstep. This is particularly useful for hard-to-find items like dried fish or specialty sauces.

- **LOCAL FARMS:** If you're looking for fresh produce, consider sourcing from local farms or co-ops that may offer organic fruits and vegetables.

- **COMMUNITY GROUPS**: Join local Filipino community groups or social media pages where members often share tips on where to find specific ingredients and may even organize bulk buying or group shopping trips.

By stocking your pantry with essential ingredients and knowing where to find them, you'll be well-equipped to explore the rich flavors of Filipino cuisine using your Instant Pot. Happy cooking!

CULTURAL CONTEXT AND PERSONAL STORIES

THE ROLE OF FOOD IN FILIPINO CULTURE

Food holds a special place in Filipino culture, serving not only as sustenance but also as a means of connection, celebration, and storytelling. The Philippines is an archipelago of diverse cultures and traditions, and this diversity is reflected in its rich culinary landscape. Here are some key points that highlight the significance of food in Filipino culture:

Family and Community: Meals are often a communal affair in Filipino culture. Families gather around the dining table to share food, stories, and laughter. This sense of togetherness fosters strong bonds and creates lasting memories. Whether it's a simple meal of Sinangag and eggs or an elaborate spread for a special occasion, the act of sharing food is integral to family life.

Celebration and Tradition: Food plays a central role in Filipino celebrations and festivals. Dishes such as Lechon (roasted pig), Pancit (noodles), and Bibingka (rice cake) are often prepared for birthdays, holidays, and significant life events. These dishes are not just about flavor; they symbolize abundance, prosperity, and the joy of coming together to celebrate.

Culinary Heritage: Filipino cuisine is a reflection of the country's history and cultural influences. From the indigenous ingredients to the Spanish, Chinese, and American influences, each dish tells a story of migration, adaptation, and resilience. Preserving traditional recipes is a way of honoring one's heritage and passing it down to future generations.

Comfort and Nurturing: Filipino food is often associated with comfort and care. Dishes like Arroz Caldo (rice porridge) and Sopas (noodle soup) are prepared for loved ones during times of illness or need, providing warmth and nourishment. Cooking and sharing these meals is an expression of love and nurturing.

Daily Life: In everyday life, Filipino food encompasses a variety of flavors and ingredients, reflecting the country's agricultural abundance. Street food vendors, local markets, and home kitchens all contribute to the vibrant food culture, making it accessible to everyone. Dishes like Kwek-Kwek (quail eggs) and Lumpiang Shanghai (spring rolls) are enjoyed as snacks or quick meals, showcasing the practicality and creativity of Filipino cooking.

PERSONAL ANECDOTES FROM JANINE'S KITCHEN

As I reflect on my culinary journey, I am reminded of the many moments in my kitchen that have shaped my love for Filipino food and the traditions that come with it. Here are a few personal anecdotes that highlight the role of food in my life:

Sunday Family Dinners: Growing up, Sunday dinners were sacred in our household. My mother would spend the entire day preparing a feast that included dishes like Adobo, Sinigang, and Pancit. The kitchen would be bustling with activity, and the aroma of simmering meats and sautéed vegetables filled the air. I remember the excitement of gathering around the table with my extended family, sharing stories, and enjoying the delicious food my mother had lovingly prepared. Those meals were about more than just food; they were about connection and love.

Learning to Cook: I learned to cook from my mother, who patiently guided me through the process of making traditional dishes. I remember standing on a stool to reach the counter, carefully measuring ingredients and stirring pots. One of my proudest moments was when I successfully made Leche Flan for the first time. The joy on my mother's face as she tasted it was priceless. Cooking with her instilled in me a deep appreciation for our culinary heritage and the importance of passing down these traditions.

Celebrating Holidays: During the Christmas season, our home would be filled with the scent of freshly baked Bibingka and Puto (steamed rice cakes). My mother would involve us in the preparation, teaching us the significance of each dish and the stories behind them. The anticipation of sharing these treats with family and friends brought a sense of joy and excitement that I still cherish today.

PERSONAL ANECDOTES FROM JANINE'S KITCHEN

Cooking for My Daughters: Now, as a mother myself, I strive to recreate those cherished moments in my kitchen. Cooking with my daughters, Katie and Lovella, has become a way to connect with them and share our culture. I love watching their faces light up as they help prepare dishes like Garlic Fried Rice or Chickpea Adobo. I tell them stories about our family traditions and the significance of each meal, hoping to instill in them the same love for cooking and appreciation for our heritage.

Food as Comfort: During challenging times, food has always been a source of comfort for me. I recall moments when I would make a pot of Arroz Caldo or Sopas whenever someone in the family was feeling under the weather. The act of cooking these nourishing dishes felt like a way to care for my loved ones, and it reminded me of my mother's love and nurturing spirit.

Through these anecdotes, I hope to convey the deep connections we forge through food and the way it shapes our identities. Cooking is not just about the ingredients; it's about the stories, the love, and the memories we create together. As you explore the recipes in this cookbook, I encourage you to embrace the traditions that resonate with you and create your own stories in the kitchen.

ADDITIONAL RESOURCES

RECOMMENDED FILIPINO COOKING BLOGS AND INFLUENCERS

To further immerse yourself in the world of Filipino cuisine, I encourage you to explore the following cooking blogs and social media influencers. These resources are filled with delicious recipes, cooking tips, and cultural insights that will inspire your culinary journey:

- **Kawaling Pinoy - KawalingPinoy.com**
A popular Filipino food blog featuring a wide array of traditional and modern recipes. The blog is known for its easy-to-follow instructions and beautiful photography.

- **The Peach Kitchen - ThePeachKitchen.com**
This blog offers a mix of Filipino and Asian-inspired recipes, along with tips for family-friendly meals. The author shares her love for cooking through engaging stories and mouthwatering dishes.

- **Filipino Food Aisle - FilipinoFoodAisle.com**
A blog dedicated to celebrating Filipino cuisine, featuring authentic recipes, cooking techniques, and cultural insights. It's a great resource for those looking to learn more about the rich culinary traditions of the Philippines.

- **Chef Jayps - Instagram: @chefjayps**
A passionate home cook and social media influencer who shares Filipino recipes and cooking tips. Follow him for delicious dishes and fun cooking videos that showcase Filipino flavors.

- **Pinoy Cooking Recipes - PinoyCookingRecipes.com**
This site provides a comprehensive collection of Filipino recipes, including traditional favorites and modern adaptations. It's an excellent resource for anyone looking to explore Filipino cooking.

RECOMMENDED FILIPINO COOKING BLOGS AND INFLUENCERS

- **Ambitious Kitchen - AmbitiousKitchen.com**

While not exclusively focused on Filipino cuisine, this blog features healthy recipes that often draw inspiration from various cultures, including Filipino dishes. It's a great resource for those looking to incorporate healthier options into their meals.

YouTube Channels

- **Filipino Food with Marc**:

A YouTube channel dedicated to Filipino cooking with easy-to-follow recipes and helpful cooking tips.

- **Chef Rob's Kitchen**:

This channel features a variety of Filipino dishes along with cooking demonstrations and techniques.

By exploring these resources, you can continue to expand your knowledge of Filipino cooking and discover new recipes that will delight your taste buds. Enjoy your culinary journey!

CONCLUSION

Celebrating Filipino Heritage
Through Cooking

As we come to the end of this journey through the vibrant world of Filipino cuisine, I hope you feel inspired to continue exploring and celebrating the rich flavors and traditions that define our culinary heritage. Cooking is more than just preparing meals; it is a way to connect with our roots, share our culture, and create lasting memories with loved ones.

Filipino food is deeply intertwined with our history, culture, and community. Each dish tells a story, from the comforting Arroz Caldo served during family gatherings to the festive Lechon enjoyed at celebrations. By preparing these dishes, you are not only nourishing your body but also honoring the generations that have come before us, who have passed down these cherished recipes and traditions.

In every recipe, you have the opportunity to infuse your own experiences and creativity, making each dish uniquely yours. Whether you are introducing Filipino flavors to your family for the first time or continuing a long-standing tradition, remember that food has the power to bring us together and foster connections that transcend time and distance.

Thank You and Encouragement
for Your Culinary Journey

Thank you for allowing me to share my passion for Filipino cooking with you. It has been a joy to guide you through the recipes, stories, and cultural insights that make our cuisine so special. Your willingness to embrace these dishes and incorporate them into your own cooking reflects the love and appreciation we all share for our heritage.

As you embark on your culinary journey, I encourage you to experiment, adapt, and make these recipes your own. Don't hesitate to explore new ingredients, try different cooking methods, and share your creations with family and friends. Cooking is a continuous learning experience, and every meal offers an opportunity to grow and discover something new.

I invite you to stay connected with the Filipino food community. Share your cooking experiences, ask questions, and seek inspiration from others who are passionate about our cuisine. Whether through social media, cooking classes, or local gatherings, the joy of cooking is best experienced together.

May your kitchen always be filled with the warmth and flavors of home, and may you create many joyful memories around the dining table. Happy cooking, and here's to celebrating the beautiful tapestry of Filipino culture through food!

Cheers!

Janine Reyes. RN

INDEX